STRESS AND DIABETES

The Underappreciated Connection

A guide to understanding
this relationship and managing the impact

STRESS AND DIABETES

The Underappreciated Connection

DR. RAJIVA GUPTA

Worldwide Published by
Pendown Press

PENDOWN PRESS

An ISO 9001 & ISO 14001 Certified Co.,

Regd. Office: 2525/193, 1st Floor, Onkar Nagar-A,

Tri Nagar, Delhi-110035

Ph.: 09350849407, 09312235086

E-mail: info@pendownpress.com

Branch Office: 1A/2A, 20, Hari Sadan, Ansari Road,

Daryaganj, New Delhi-110002

Ph.: 011-45794768

Website: PendownPress.com

First Edition: 2023

ISBN: 978-93-5554-470-4

Layout and Cover Designed by Pendown Graphics Team

Printed and Bound in India by Thomson Press India Ltd.

I dedicate the book to my family and friends, who gave me unwavering encouragement to follow my passion for writing the book.

Contents

Chapter 6

Chapter 7

Acknowledgement

I always wanted to write a book but found the task a formidable one. I am eternally grateful to my family: my wife Alka, my children Ishan and Divya, who said, "Rajiva, you want to write a book, go ahead". My little 4 years plus grandson who taught me how to be stress-free with the mantra "study, play, laugh and sleep".

I thank my patients, who made me realize that diabetes treatment is not just control of blood glucose levels and preventing medical complications but also about addressing psychological issues and stress that they face on a daily basis. They taught me that their problems are beyond drugs and lifestyle.

The publication of this book would not have been possible without the support of Dinesh Verma and his wonderful team at the Pendown Press.

I am thankful to Anita Verma for her valuable suggestions whenever sought from her.

I am indebted to my teachers in the medical college who taught me not only the science but the art of medicine.

Chapter 1

Introduction
to Stress and Diabetes

"Why have I developed diabetes? How will my life change now? I am struggling with my sugar fluctuations. There is nothing left in my life except thinking about what to eat and how much to exercise. I am fed up."

One can feel the stress that these words convey; the stress that a person faces upon being diagnosed with diabetes or during the management of diabetes.

Diabetes is rising at an alarming rate in India.

It is disturbing to note that only about 1/4th of the patients out of 7.7 crore patients with diabetes in India achieve glucose control as well as a good quality of life. (International Diabetes Federation data 2019).

Along with diabetes, stress too is on the rise in India.

(An excerpt from TIMESOFINDIA.COM:
Created Feb 22, 2021, 21:00 IST)

"82% of Indians are stressed out today. Stress has become an overheard word in our lives."

There is a definite connection between stress and illness.

Stress has been identified as one of the most important determinants of emotional health.

Stress is defined as a state of mental or emotional strain or tension resulting from adverse or very demanding circumstances.

(Oxford Dictionary)

Stress is of 2 types

- **Acute stress:** is short-term stress that occurs in response to a specific event or situation and goes away once the situation is over. The body releases hormones like cortisol and adrenaline. These make one alert and ready to act. This response is called a "fight or flight" response. It can be helpful as it enables the person to deal with the situation. Examples: taking a test or meeting a deadline.

  However, if the factor leading to stress is not resolved, it can lead to negative consequences in the form of physical changes like aches and pains, diarrhea, constipation, nausea, dizziness, chest pain, rapid heartbeat etc., and emotional changes like anxiety, irritability, feeling low, sad, excessive worry etc.

- **Chronic stress:** persists for weeks or months. It can be caused by factors like work, relationships, and financial problems, daily pressures, losing a job, losing a dear one or other unhappy life events. Often one becomes used to it and ignores addressing it as a problem. Chronic stress manifests in emotional and physical symptoms (fatigue, irritability, difficulty in sleeping, difficulty in concentration, feeling lonely or isolated, neglect of responsibilities etc.), and then it results in distress. Chronic stress can trigger health problems like heart disease, high blood pressure, and mental health disorders like depression, anxiety etc.

The Stress Response

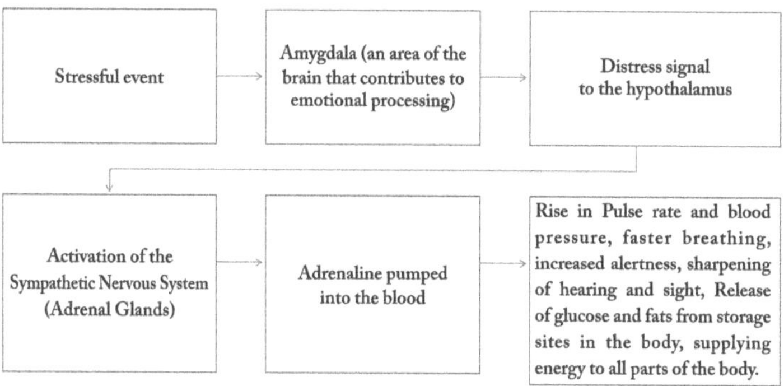

Overview of Diabetes

Diabetes Mellitus is a long-term medical condition in which the body is unable to regulate blood sugar (glucose) levels.

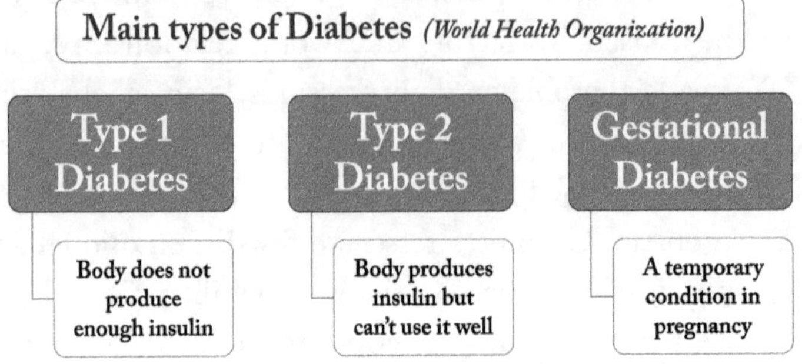

There are three main types of diabetes:

- **Type 1 diabetes** is an autoimmune disorder in which the body's immune system attacks and destroys the cells in the pancreas that produce insulin, a hormone that helps regulate blood sugar levels. It is more common in children, teens, or young adults. Daily injections of insulin are needed to manage this type of diabetes.

- **Type 2 diabetes** accounts for 90% of all diabetes. It most often occurs in adulthood, but because of high obesity rates, children and teens too are now being diagnosed with diabetes. Here the body stops responding to insulin, and over time, the pancreas does not make enough insulin. Not all people with type 2 diabetes are overweight or obese.

- **Gestational diabetes (GDM)** develops in a pregnant woman who does not already have diabetes. It usually resolves after the woman delivers her baby. However, such women are at increased risk for developing type 2 diabetes later in life.

Criteria for Diagnosis of Diabetes
(American Diabetes Association)

Fasting ⩾ (more than or equal to) 126 mg/dl

2 Hours Post meal ⩾ 200 mg/dl

A1c values of ⩾ 6.5% (A1c tells about the average
blood sugar for the past 2 to 3 months).

What are the complications of diabetes?

If not properly managed, diabetes can lead to several health problems like heart attacks, brain stroke, kidney disease, damage to the nerves, particularly in the feet, leading to pain, tingling, and loss of feeling, eye diseases resulting in reduced vision, complications in women with GDM, inflammation of the gums and increased risk of infections.

Why should diabetes be treated?

It is imperative to treat diabetes in order to prevent diabetes-related complications and achieve a good quality of life.

How to best achieve the goals of the treatment of diabetes?

*The foundation of treatment is based on following
a healthy lifestyle and maintaining psychological
well-being to achieve diabetes treatment goals.*

(American Diabetes Association, 2023)

We all know that good glucose control decreases the risks of future complications. People with diabetes need support to engage in healthy behaviors (lifestyle and treatment) in order to achieve optimal glucose control, prevent complications and have a good quality of life.

1. **Lifestyle management**

    a. Nutrition/dietary management

    b. Physical activity/exercise

    c. Healthy sleep pattern and duration

    d. Counseling on quitting smoking where needed

2. **Treatment and maintenance**

    a. Adherence to taking medicines (Insulin and oral medication) as advised

    b. Blood glucose monitoring

    c. Physician visits as advised

3. **Emotional health**

    Diabetes self-management is demanding and requires considerable discipline. It is more than a physical condition. Also, living with diabetes negatively affects emotional well-being and quality of life. Often emotional and mental problems are associated with uncontrolled sugar levels, diabetes-related complications and reduced quality of life.

Chapter 2

What is the Connection between Stress and Diabetes?

"My visit to the doctor for my Diabetes consultations is often a one-way communication. I am told that my sugar levels are high, and few medicines are added or changed. There is no effort to find out how I am managing my diabetes, how worried I may be about it, or whether my stress contributes to the high sugar value.

I wish if someone talked to me about these things, it would make me feel that the doctor is genuinely interested in me as a person and that they accept that it's fine for me to have these concerns and anxieties and fears and feelings."

~RK 39 years female (type 2 Diabetes since 10 years)

*"I'm worried about my future. I fear my kidneys or eyes
will get affected. I get sleepless nights thinking and
worrying about the chance of my daughter getting diabetes
and becoming a burden on my loved ones. I am scared.
Diabetes is scary. It is not just a condition of values . It is
an unpleasant chapter of my present and my future life."*

~SP, 43 years male (recently detected with Type 2 Diabetes)

Stress and diabetes are related in several ways. Stress can trigger the onset of diabetes as well as disturb the control of blood sugar in diabetes. People with diabetes are more likely to experience stress due to the burden of managing their condition and other factors.

Emotional health is considered an important part of the care of patients with diabetes.

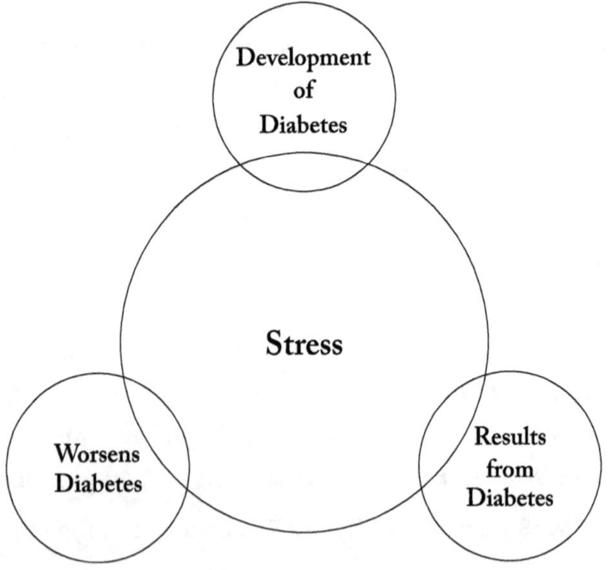

Despite this, the connection between stress and diabetes continues to be under appreciated.

Does stress trigger the onset of diabetes/cause diabetes?

Yes, stress can contribute to the development of Type 2 and Gestational diabetes mellitus.

Type 2 Diabetes: can be triggered by very stressful life events, a history of childhood neglect, work-related stress, sleep disorders (OSA-Obstructive Sleep Apnea), sleep disturbance etc.

Post Gestational Type 2 Diabetes Mellitus: The chances of Type 2 Diabetes after GDM are high. The reasons may be:

- The stress caused by concerns regarding the well-being of the fetus, method of delivery, future diabetes risk in the baby and the mother etc.

- The emotional distress coming in the way of subsequent follow-ups and prevention of Post GDM Type 2 Diabetes Mellitus.

Case-in-Point

BR, 42-year male. Recently diagnosed with Type 2 Diabetes Mellitus despite a healthy lifestyle. His mother has diabetes. He is not overweight and follows a healthy lifestyle. He has a lot of work-related stress.

Gestational Diabetes Mellitus

PW 34-year female, pregnancy duration 20 weeks, past h/o pregnancy loss, currently conceived after IVF (In vitro fertilization). Had a lot of anxiety regarding the outcome of the pregnancy.

Conclusion: Emotional stress and anxiety are contributory factors for the development of type 2 diabetes and GDM.

Does diabetes cause stress?

Several studies have confirmed what many healthcare professionals and people with diabetes have known for years:

- That diabetes causes multiple psychological problems.

- That the psychological issues pose barriers to achieving adequate glucose control.

- That these interfere with the implementation of a healthy lifestyle.

Excerpt from a blog

"I care a great deal about my health. There will be times when it seems that I don't care. But I do care. Sometimes, though, it is just overwhelming and exhausting. I want you to remember that I am doing the best I can at every moment."

Stress is the most important factor underlying the emotional health of a person with diabetes. Living with diabetes creates an emotional burden on the person with diabetes, now being recognized as Diabetes Distress.

Living with diabetes is a challenge in which the person with diabetes is involved in a lifelong integration of demanding and complex tasks (lifestyle changes and medicines). Despite their best efforts, freedom from short and long-term problems may still not be attained.

The stress results from:

- The rigid daily management (food, weight, medication, repeated finger pricks/blood samples for monitoring of blood glucose, exercises).

- Fear of complications such as heart disease or nerve or kidney disease.

- Feelings of guilt and anxiety when results go off track.

- Episodes of hypoglycemia, i.e. low blood sugar levels and high sugar.

- Social impact of diabetes (e.g., stigma, discrimination, lack of support or understanding by others)

- Financial problems.
- Disturbed relationships with health professionals, family, or friends.

Diabetes distress has been reported in:

- 25% of people with type 1 diabetes
- 20% with insulin-treated type 2 diabetes
- 10% with non-insulin treated type 2 diabetes

How does diabetes distress impact the management of diabetes?

- Poor self-management (e.g., reduced physical activity, less healthy eating, not taking medication as recommended, less frequent monitoring of blood glucose, and smoking)
- Poor sugar control and high A1C
- Hypoglycemia and hyperglycemia (low and high sugar fluctuations). *Termed Brittle diabetes refers to a condition in which persons with diabetes experiences frequent and severe fluctuations in their blood sugar. This can make it difficult to manage the condition. The underlying factors are mainly related to stress, family maladjustments, etc.*

> **Case-in-Point**
>
> *RS, a 37 year female, Type 2 diabetes for 10 years, repeated episodes of hypo and hyperglycemia. Multiple stressors. Suggested relaxation techniques and yoga, which helped.*

- More and earlier onset of complications.

- Decreased quality of life and social interactions.

- Intense changes to self-management (e.g., more frequent blood glucose monitoring) themselves increase distress.

- Decreased general and emotional well-being.

- Negative impact on relationships with family members and friends.

- Symptoms of anxiety, depression

    - Diabetes distress involves emotional symptoms that overlap with depression. Despite their similarities, depression and diabetes distress are different. Diabetes distress is an expected reaction to diabetes, whereas depression refers to how people feel about their life in general.

What is Diabetes Burnout ?

- Diabetes burnout is a state of physical or emotional exhaustion caused by the continuous burden of diabetes and efforts to manage it. The individual feels that despite their best efforts, their blood glucose levels are erratic and unpredictable. They get disappointed with the results. They start exhibiting unhealthy behavior like skipping insulin doses, not monitoring blood glucose, unhealthy eating..

- These individuals are sometimes labelled as being "tough," "uncooperative, demotivated despite their best efforts to manage their diabetes.

- People with diabetes burnout understand the importance of managing diabetes well for their better health but feel unable to connect with management of their diabetes. They get frustrated . "I've tried everything but it didn't work"; "I stopped doing blood sugar check with the glucometer because I know it's not going to be good."

Therefore it is important to regularly watch for signs of distress to prevent the adverse impact on health, prevent mild stress getting complicated to depression/diabetes burnout so that the physician can offer timely assistance to address concerns as they arise.

Chapter 3

What are the Strategies for Reducing the Impact of Stress on Health in Diabetes?

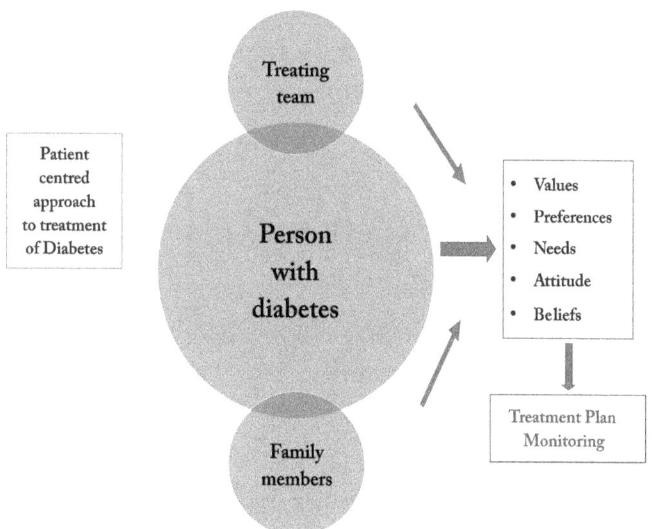

An understanding of the relationship between diabetes and stress will help us minimize the impact in a more effective manner. The approach of the doctor treating the person with diabetes plays a crucial role in the effective management of stress.

The responsibility of the doctor is enormous and is shared in detail below.

The Responsibility of the Doctor

- Remember to put yourself in their shoes and think about what it would be like to manage diabetes 24/7.

- Ask about stress at every appointment to explore the impact of diabetes on daily life and well-being and how they are doing with their diabetes. Diabetes distress fluctuates over time as life circumstances can change quickly. Do not wait for deterioration in control or psychological status to occur. Quick, proactive action results in an improvement in diabetes control, lowering the risk of complications and fosters better psychological well-being.

- Explain the signs and impact of stress on their daily management and well-being and emphasize that it is a common phenomenon.

- If a person blames oneself, explain that diabetes outcomes do not reflect who they are as a person; diabetes does not define one as being "good" or "bad" or a failure. Instead assure them that managing diabetes is a difficult task and that they should focus on what they are doing, despite less than ideal outcomes.

- Use non-judgmental and encouraging language, e.g. rather than referring to an A1C value as "good" or "bad" or talking about "correcting" blood sugar, approach their daily blood glucose values or A1C simply as data and "adjust" rather than "correct" their blood sugar.

- The patients may be encouraged to ask questions pertaining to fear of complications, side effects of medications, and misconceptions, e.g. insulin increases complications of diabetes or damages the kidneys.

These questions offer the person an opportunity to

- Express any difficulties (emotional, behavioral, or social) that they are facing, and express how particular diabetes-related issues are causing them distress and interfering with their self-care and/or their life in general. They may help minimize negative emotions about diabetes.

- Identify the most difficult part of living with diabetes (the sticking point). This identification makes it easier to help people solve a problem they face. The clinician can also help them identify the most effective ways to get unstuck by first seeking their options.

- Tell them to do one thing at a time. This helps to decrease the feeling of being overwhelmed. Ask them to make a list and work on each task separately, one at a time.

- Ask them to choose a comfortable pace: As one works on goals, like increasing physical activity, it is best to take it slowly. The goal may be to walk 50 minutes each day, but they can start by walking 15 minutes a day or every other day and then gradually increase it.

- Assist in finding options to minimize costs of medicines and consumables, e.g. generic medicines through government programs.

- Suggest taking a safe break

    - It is unrealistic to expect people with diabetes to monitor their health 24/7.

    - Enabling them the freedom to take short breaks occasionally will help maintain motivation to take good care of their health in the long term.

    - For example, if they are struggling to check their blood glucose several times a day, consider reducing the number of pricks for a short time.

Remind the person that you understand managing diabetes is a full-time job and that it's okay to take a break once in a while.

- Remain supportive and encouraging. This will eliminate any feelings of guilt that the person may be experiencing for not managing their diabetes "perfectly."

- If away from goals, don't criticize but appreciate the effort. Appreciation builds motivation. The focus should be on action, i.e. what people are doing. The results will follow. Express that no plan ever works perfectly.

- Diabetes management is a life situation to be seen as a series of experiments. The success lies in experimenting with making diabetes care easier and more effective and using the results of each experiment to plan further refinements and solve new problems as they arise.

- The plan the doctor and the patient first put together is based on the best information available at the time, which needs to be tested for the results. Acknowledging this reality from the start can help prevent the disappointment and discouragement that many patients and doctors feel when a plan does not work perfectly.

Steps to be taken by the person with diabetes

Have a support system in place to help you manage your stress and overall health.

- **Talk with your family and friends:** Their support plays a crucial role in maintaining lifestyle changes and facilitating diabetes management. They can remind you to take your medicines, help monitor your blood sugar levels and join you in being physically active. They can also learn more about diabetes and accompany you on your visit to the doctor.

Family support has been shown to have a positive impact on adherence to treatment, healthy diet, and exercise, reducing the stressful impact of illness, improving psychological well-being, and better glucose control. Sharing your thoughts and feelings can help reduce stress and improve your sense of well-being.

- **Diabetes burdens everyone who lives with, loves and cares for someone who has diabetes.** The way the family members adapt to the person with diabetes may either help or hinder the management of diabetes. Their involvement may vary from being supportive to exercising excessive control and totally ignoring diabetes.

They may fail to understand the feelings of the patient, indulge in nagging criticism and impose excessive food restrictions. This makes the person further stressed and isolated, decreasing compliance with treatment and resulting in worsening of control. There may be a breakdown of the communication:

  - The family members may avoid healthy discussions with the patient.

  - The patient may stop communication with the family members thinking that it may make them uncomfortable.

> ## Cases-in-point
>
> *RK is a 56-year lady with DM for 12 years. Hba1c 10.7% FBG 240 mg/dl PPBG 370 mg/dl. No exercise. Chronic Kidney Disease. On Insulin + oral medicines.*
>
> *Reason: She becomes stressed when relatives talk with her about things she doesn't like, and her sugar shoots up.*
>
> *Pooja is a 34-year female with a 4-month-old baby. The control deteriorated about 2 weeks back.*
>
> *Reason: Suddenly, she was overwhelmed by domestic work, which created stress, and her self-management of diabetes suffered.*

- **Talk to other people with diabetes.** They may understand what you are going through. Ask them how they deal with their diabetes and what works for them. They can help you feel less lonely and overwhelmed.

- **Take time to do things you enjoy.** Set aside time in your day to do something you really love e.g. hobbies or being with friends.

- **Stay organized, make a to-do list and manage time effectively.**

- **Set boundaries on your time and energy. Say NO when you have to.**

- Have adequate sleep.

- Relaxation techniques like deep breathing, yoga and meditation can help calm the mind and body.

- Mindfulness involves focusing on the present moment and paying attention to your thoughts, feelings and surroundings without judgment.

Don't be too harsh with yourself. Remember that the management of diabetes is a journey with ups and downs. If things go off track, compliment yourself on the progress you have made.

Pay attention to your feelings. It's important to take care of your mental and emotional health along with your physical health. Everybody reacts differently to stress. Finding which stress management strategy works best for you is a matter of trial and error. Practice these regularly.

If you notice that you're feeling frustrated, tired, and unable to make decisions about your diabetes care, reach out to your family, friends, and healthcare provider for support.

Chapter 4

Facing the Diagnosis of Diabetes

The diagnosis of diabetes is perhaps the most disturbing and stressful time for an individual and their family. It is the turning point where one has to accept the reality of managing a lifelong and demanding condition, which obviously no one chooses to have.

The person may feel that life will not be the same as it was before diagnosis and fears a loss of independence and health.

The initial emotional reactions can be of shock, disbelief, anger, self-blame, anxiety and denial. The people in denial cover up their fear by avoidance. They reason that since no symptoms are there, the diagnosis may be wrong. The denial results in unfavorable health outcomes because of the delay in starting treatment and lifestyle modification.

There may be questions such as, "Can it be cured? Do I have to take drugs throughout my life? What does it mean for my long-term health? How will it affect my everyday life?"

- **The reactions are genuine if we consider that:**
  - A person with type 1 diabetes
    - ❖ Does almost 100 finger pricks (average four per day) in a month
    - ❖ Has repeated episodes of hypoglycemia
    - ❖ Always making diabetes related decisions daily
    - ❖ Feels exhausted of thinking about diabetes
    - ❖ Feels that their family is continually concerned about their diabetes and welfare.
  - A person with type 2 diabetes is expected to change the habits (healthier eating, more exercise, and losing weight) that have developed over a lifetime. One has to make choices at every meal (e.g., continually resisting their favorite foods and forcibly eating foods that are not tasteful.
- A person can feel overwhelmed by the plethora of information and the multiple tasks (medication taking, monitoring of blood glucose, dietary changes, physical activity, regular health check-ups) to learn. These may put extra pressure posing a barrier in carrying on the tasks.

How should we minimize the impact and assist the person with newly diagnosed diabetes?

Here again, the doctor plays a very crucial role, as detailed below.

- **The Responsibility of the Doctor**
    - We should communicate with the person thinking about how we would have felt if we were diagnosed with diabetes. It will help the person with diabetes realize we are "on their side".

    - The first interaction between the patient, the treating physician and the family members lays the foundation of a trustful relationship which ultimately results in good outcomes.

    - Acknowledge the daily challenges of living with diabetes and the efforts it takes to manage the condition are natural.

    - Living with and managing diabetes is a learning process, often with "trial and error" and ups and downs. Provide emotional support

    - Ask people to make changes to their lifestyle with respect, hope, empathy, and understanding while being factual and informative.

    - It is important to avoid using threat and creating fear during consultations about management of diabetes.

    - Answer questions about all concerns and for providing the person with diabetes with accurate information about diabetes and its treatment.

–   Tell them that the condition can be managed effectively and complications are not inevitable, indeed. While untreated diabetes is the leading cause of many complications, well-managed diabetes leads to a life free from complications.

–   As health professionals, we may have expert knowledge about diabetes, but we should also acknowledge that only the person with diabetes has expertise about their own diabetes and their own life. It is our responsibility to tell the person, "Over time, you will become an expert in managing your diabetes."

–   We should encourage them to share their thoughts initially and at regular intervals during the first year after diagnosis about how they are coping, self-management, and the impact of diabetes on their daily life. We should also try to understand why they may not be making changes that would appear to be "good" for them and help them to identify the reasons and whether they can find ways to overcome them.

Chapter 5

Facing Complications/Transitions/ Special Situations in Diabetes

Complications

It is known that complications often result from poor control. The onset of complications increases emotional distress and causes deterioration of quality of life.

> ### Case-in-Point
>
> *DV 59-year male, DM since 25 years Hba1c 9.8% FBG 240 mg/dl PPBG 450 mg/dl. No exercise. Peripheral neuropathy (numbness in feet). He is on Insulin + oral medicines.*
>
> *Attendants: Does not monitor and does not share stresses. They feel that he probably has work-related stress.*

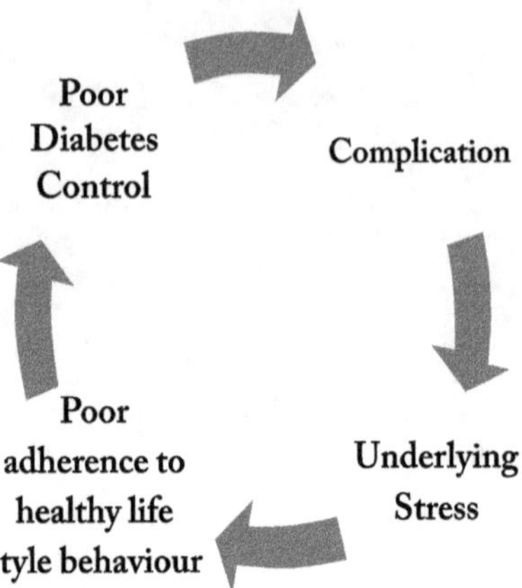

Steps to reduce the impact of stress include encouragement to follow the new treatment plan in order to prevent further complications, assist in managing blood sugar by adjusting insulin/other medicines and lifestyle management (healthy diet, exercise, enough sleep).

- The doctor should offer emotional support to let them know that the doctor cares.

- Involve the family for support.

Stress in transitions: Times of transition are challenging for people with diabetes. A few examples are the transition of age groups (childhood to adolescence, adolescence to adulthood, adulthood to elderly age group), marriage, becoming a parent, divorce, loss of employment, change of residence, retirement etc. Any disruption in treatment should be minimized by providing emotional support to the person with diabetes and their family members and encouraging them to plan ahead, if feasible.

Special Populations

Stress in adolescents and children with diabetes: They may worry about the impact of their disease on their future and feel isolated and different from their peers, which can lead to social and emotional challenges. The parents should encourage the child to talk about their feelings and concerns related to diabetes. This can help them feel heard and supported.

Case-in-Point

SK, a 15-year-old school-going child, was detected with Type 1 diabetes just about 2 weeks before the consultation. This period was very crucial in view of academics, health, emotional balance and daily life. The medical and academic aspects were discussed with SK and his parents. On follow-ups, he is more cheerful, able to manage his blood glucose effectively and participates in various activities in the school. The parents are also more relaxed.

Stress in the elderly with diabetes

Older adults with diabetes may experience stress due to limitations in physical and mental capabilities, lack of social support and resulting loneliness and isolation. It is important for older adults with diabetes to seek support from friends, family, and healthcare professionals.

> ## Case-in-Point
>
> *Mr. RR, 74, having diabetes for 35 years. Reported repeated episodes of low sugar (hypoglycemia) followed by loss of consciousness and being rushed to the hospital.*

Family members revealed that he was lately becoming forgetful and missing meals. The family was very upset. Mr. RR, too, was upset. This is what he said, "Dr., I don't know what happens all of a sudden?"

A caretaker was arranged for, and the medicines were modified to decrease the intensity of treatment; the family members were counseled to encourage physical activity within his capacity.

It worked; Mr. RR departed just about a year ago after a fruitful life of 92 years.

Stress in pregnancy with diabetes

Women with diabetes may worry about potential complications like preterm birth or birth defects in the baby. Pregnancy can cause fluctuations in blood sugar levels, which can be difficult to manage. They may need to monitor their blood sugar levels more frequently and make adjustments to their insulin or medication regimen.

Case-in-Point

SD 31-year-old primi gravida, pregnancy 7 weeks, was detected with diabetes before pregnancy but well controlled. Now the control has deteriorated.

She was counseled about regular blood sugar monitoring, physical activity and diet, as well as emotional health. She was suggested to get enough rest, eat a healthy diet, and engage in exercise (within limits as discussed with the Obstetrician) and relaxation techniques such as deep breathing or meditation.

Chapter 6

Other Sources
of Stress in Diabetes

In addition to the situations, discussed earlier, diabetes brings along with it other stressors, such as:

- Fear of Hypoglycemia (Low blood sugar)
- Fear of Hyperglycemia (High blood sugar)
- Fear of injections, needles and finger pricks

Fear of Hypoglycemia:

- Fear of hypoglycemia is the fear evoked by the risk and/or occurrence of hypoglycemia (low blood glucose).
- Hypoglycemia is caused by relative insulin excess in the absence of sufficient blood glucose.
- If not detected and treated, glucose continues to fall, resulting in very low blood glucose levels, leading to serious complications like loss of consciousness.

- Being concerned about hypoglycemia is appropriate so long as it keeps a person attentive and responsive to hypoglycemic symptoms to enable timely treatment. However, if the concern becomes excessive, it may have a negative impact causing:
    - Impaired quality of life
    - Emotional disturbance
    - Impaired ability to manage diabetes with high a1c and more complications
    - Reluctance to use insulin in future (if necessary)
    - Effect on family members' quality of life (disturbance in their sleep or their constant worry about the person's safety when alone)
- **Underlying factors for fear of hypoglycemia:**
    - A side-effect of glucose-lowering medications (e.g., insulin and certain oral drugs).
    - Previous experience with hypoglycemia.
    - Limited understanding of hypoglycemia and skills in preventing, recognizing, and treating it can cause more frequent and severe hypoglycemic episodes, which in turn can trigger fear of hypoglycemia.
    - People who have impaired awareness of hypoglycemia, i.e. they fail to recognize the beginning of hypoglycemia. The brain, already deficient in glucose before recognition, makes

it more difficult for the person to notice falling blood glucose and take corrective action. Unawareness aggravates fear as well as poses a future risk of hypoglycemia.

– People with anxiety.

The relationship between anxiety and fear of hypoglycemia is two-sided (bi-directional)

A person with anxiety may be distracted and miss out on recognizing hypoglycemic symptoms, increasing their risk of a low blood glucose level

The experience of recurrent severe hypoglycemia may induce fear and anxiety in people who were not previously anxious

The symptoms of hypoglycemia (e.g., tremors, sweating, and palpitations) are similar to anxiety symptoms. This overlap can hinder interpretation and appropriate treatment of a falling blood glucose level.

What are the fears in the minds of patients regarding hypoglycemia?

Fear of losing consciousness in public/home, having an accident/injury or the very worst (but rare) scenario of sudden death.

How to identify fear of hypoglycemia

- "Over-compensatory behaviors" like taking less insulin than needed

- Frequent snacking

- "Avoidance behaviors"

    - Limiting physical or social activities

    - Acceptance of persistently high blood glucose levels

    - Reluctance in implementing treatment changes to lower blood glucose levels.

What are the strategies to minimize fear of hypoglycemia?

The Responsibility of the Doctor

- Specifically, ask about fear and occurrence of hypoglycemia on each visit.

- Explain symptoms, reasons, mechanisms and treatment of hypoglycemia.

- Assure them that severe episodes are experienced by a minority of people with diabetes, and many of these can be prevented.

- Educate them that effective and timely treatment of hypoglycemia is crucial because of the small window of opportunity to respond before awareness and judgment may be compromised.

- Agree on a blood glucose target range that is both safe and comfortable for the person, with the understanding that this "individualized" target may be higher than the standard targets.

- The "Start low, go slow" approach to start with lower doses and gradually increase them to lower blood glucose levels in order to minimize their fear and restore awareness of hypoglycemia symptoms.

Fear of Hyperglycemia (High blood sugar)

- Fear of high sugar may be caused by worrying about the future and the possibility of diabetes complications, experiencing unpleasant symptoms of high blood glucose levels (fatigue, lethargy, frequent urination), and fearing diabetic ketoacidosis.

- A person may respond to their fear of hyperglycemia by keeping their blood glucose levels (too) low, resulting in an increased risk of recurrent hypoglycemia. In turn, this will increase their likelihood of impaired awareness of hypoglycemic symptoms (due to recurrent hypoglycemia) and their risk of adverse consequences of undetected hypoglycemic episodes.

- Continually correcting blood glucose levels with extra insulin or food out of distress or anxiety upon seeing high blood sugar values.

The Responsibility of the Doctor

- Shifting the focus from scary information about complications to the maintenance of blood glucose in optimal ranges is more assuring and does not create anxiety.

- Ask which complication are they most fearful of. Having a family member with diabetes complications can exaggerate the individual's perception of their own risk.

- Assure them that diabetes complications are avoidable and not every person with diabetes develops complications if sugar is well controlled.

- Assure them that the complications have reduced considerably in recent years due to more effective, modern diabetes treatments and technologies.

- Emphasize that perfect blood glucose levels do not exist and that minor fluctuations will have little impact. It is the persistently elevated glucose levels (over long periods of time) that place a person at higher risk of developing complications, and it is the average blood glucose which is the parameter known to be important in determining long-term complications.

Fear of injections, needles and finger pricks

- Suggesting the use of insulin may evoke anxiety and fear of needles, injections, and finger pricks.

- These can contribute to delays in starting insulin, which in turn, affects diabetes outcomes (e.g., elevated A1C and greater risk of long-term diabetes complications along with worsening of emotional well-being).

- Surprisingly, these negative feelings about starting or intensifying insulin may be present despite being aware of the benefits of insulin.

- 1 in 4 people with type 2 diabetes for whom insulin is clinically indicated is "not at all willing" to start insulin.

- 1 in 10 people with type 2 diabetes using insulin is dissatisfied with it.

- Concerns about insulin among people with type 2 diabetes can be grouped into the following themes

  - **Concerns/anxieties/fears about medications**

    - Doubts about the effectiveness or dependence on insulin

    - Possible side effects (e.g., weight gain or hypoglycemia)

    - Fear of injections, needles, or pain

  - **Perceptions about using insulin**

    - Lack of confidence/skills (e.g., in their ability to use insulin, coping with a complex regimen, or injecting in public)

- ❖ Impact on self-perception and life (e.g., feelings of personal failure or self-blame for needing insulin

- ❖ Injections interfering with daily activities or social stigma

- ❖ Fears about diabetes progression (e.g., insulin as a sign that diabetes is "getting worse," insulin as the "last resort.")

- ❖ Mistaken beliefs that insulin leads to diabetes complications.

How to remove the fear?

The Responsibility of the Doctor

- Address the causes of fear and education about the reason, teaching injecting insulin and checking blood glucose. Demonstrate that modern insulin pens, finer needles and lancets all help to minimize the pain of insulin injections and blood glucose checks.

- Assist in taking decisions by telling the positives. Make it clear that it is the individual's decision whether or not to use insulin. However, you would certainly like to assist them in making an informed choice.

- Explain the natural course and progressive nature of type 2 diabetes and the likelihood that their treatment will change over time.

- Emphasize that needing insulin does not indicate their failure and that insulin is simply the best treatment option to meet their body's needs right now.

  - is a powerful way to control blood glucose within target range to prevent long-term complications

  - allows for more flexibility with food and planning of meals

  - improves their energy levels

- Demonstrate the Insulin Injection process

  - First, show the person an insulin pen, and the size of the needle. They may be surprised to see how small the needle is.

  - Second Step is to demonstrate the process of taking an injection, to show how simple it is.

  - Third invite the person to try an injection for themselves, during the consultation with you.

This process helps a person to realize that injecting insulin is not as difficult or as painful as they imagined it would be

- **"Insulin Trial"**

  - A time-bound "insulin trial" is a way to encourage the person to "experiment" with insulin for a period of time that both agree on.

- As an example, a one-month "trial" may be started for a person to experience how they can fit an insulin regimen into their lifestyle. If they are comfortable with that, extending the "trial" to three months will enable them to notice improvements in the sugar control.

- Make sure the person feels confident that they have the option of reverting back to their previous treatment if this experiment has not worked out for them.

- At the end of the experiment review their experience and discuss if they feel it is beneficial for them.

• Advise that insulin use may begin with just one or two injections per day.

Case-in-Point

Patient CK, a 35-year female, suggested using insulin.

Expressed a lot of worry and fear. Used to think, "I was a failure; my disease has progressed, and I wasn't looking after myself properly."

She was made to talk with other people. Peer support helped her to change her view. The perspective shifted to this, "I started to think of needing insulin as another option to manage diabetes."

Chapter 7

Mental Health Problems in Diabetes

Clinically significant mental health problems are more prevalent in people with diabetes than in those without.

- Depression

- Anxiety

- Disordered Eating Behavior

- Sleep Disorders

Diabetes and Depression

Depression or Diabetes Distress?

- Depression is often confused with diabetes distress.

- Depression can influence how people feel about living with diabetes, but it is broader, affecting how they feel about life in general.

- Conversely, diabetes distress is the emotional distress arising specifically from living with and managing diabetes and does not necessarily affect how people feel about their life in general.

- While diabetes distress and depression are separate entities, each is a risk factor for the other, meaning people with depression are more likely to develop diabetes distress and vice versa.

Prevalence

- None to low levels of Distress/Depression 50-70%
- Significant Diabetes Distress   20-30%
- Significant distress + Depression   5-15%
- Significant Depression   5-10%
- Major depression is a psychological condition indicated by a persistent state of sadness or depressed mood and/or lack of interest and pleasure in usual activities.

- Past and current depression are risk factors for the development of type 2 diabetes, especially if the individual has other risk factors such as obesity and a family history of type 2 diabetes.

- Diabetes distress and complications are risk factors for depression in patients with diabetes.

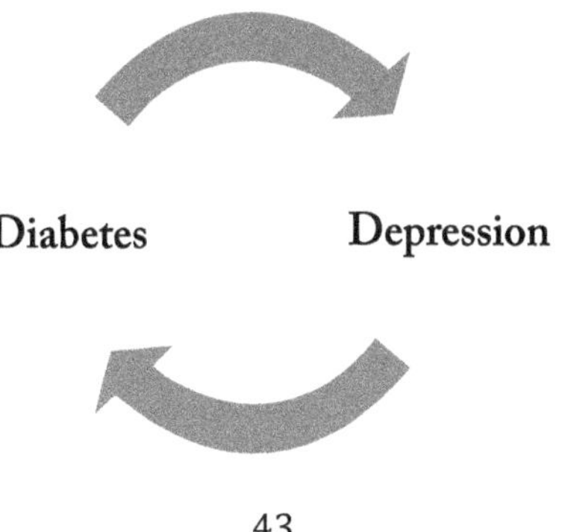

- Women have higher rates of depression than men.

- In people with diabetes, depression or depressive symptoms are associated with adverse medical and psychological outcomes like reduced physical activity, less healthy eating, not taking medication as recommended, less frequent self-monitoring of blood glucose and high A1C.

- Hypoglycemia and hyperglycemia (Glucose level fluctuations).

- Increased prevalence and earlier onset of complications.

- Risk factor for premature mortality.

- Increased risk of diabetes distress
    - Elevated anxiety symptoms
    - Impaired quality of life and social functioning

- People with coexisting depressive and anxiety symptoms are likely to experience greater emotional impairment and take longer to recover.

- Some depressive symptoms overlap with symptoms of diabetes (e.g., fatigue, sleep disturbance, changes in weight, and altered eating habits).

- Depression can be treated effectively (with psychological therapies and medications).

- Relieving depression often infuses positive feelings, behaviors, and better metabolic outcomes.

- Prominent depressive symptoms and mild depression also need attention, as they can develop into major depression.

The Responsibility of the Doctor

- Ask about diabetes-specific and other life circumstances

- Suggest regular exercise

- Refer to a mental health professional (psychotherapist/ psychiatrist)

Diabetes and Anxiety

- An anxiety disorder is a psychological condition indicated by frequent, intense, and excessive worry, occurring for at least six months and substantially affecting daily functioning resulting in significant distress.

- Affects one in five people with diabetes.

- Anxiety symptoms in people with diabetes are associated with difficulty in controlling blood sugar, diabetes complications, depressive symptoms and impaired quality of life

- It may be difficult to recognize, as severe anxiety and panic attacks share some symptoms with hypoglycemia (e.g., sweating, increased heart rate, tremors).

- Situations of elevated anxiety symptoms specific to diabetes

  - Occurrence or fear of hypoglycemia

  - Not meeting blood glucose targets

- Initiation of insulin injections

- Onset of complications

- Psychotherapy and/or drugs can help decrease anxiety in people with diabetes.

Diet and Eating Problems

"What should I eat? What should I avoid?"

Managing a specific diet adds to the stress of diabetes. In fact, the most challenging part of diabetes management is what to eat.

- There is not a "one-size-fits-all" eating pattern. The diet should be individualized based on requirements, lifestyles and preferences.

- The pleasure of eating should be maintained by providing neutral messages about food choices and limiting food choices ONLY when indicated by scientific evidence.

- The person with diabetes may be flexible. It is okay to dine out occasionally or go partying. Being too strict can lead to frustration.

- Motivate the person by reminding them that eating a healthy diet helps better control diabetes and overall better health.

- However, excessive preoccupation with diet can result in disordered eating behavior swinging between severe dietary restrictions, such as severely limiting calories or eliminating essential nutrients from one's diet to control blood sugar/weight and compulsive and excessive eating.

- On the contrary, the psychological burden of diabetes management can itself lead to low mood and distress, which results in the individual's inability to control their hunger and satiety and uncontrolled eating.

- About one in five people with diabetes exhibit DEB (Disordered Eating Behavior).

- Binge eating/night eating syndrome are the most common forms of disordered eating behaviors in type 2 Diabetes

  - Binge eating involves eating an unusually large amount of food in a short period of time due to feelings of being out of control.

  - Binge eating doesn't often come to light due to guilt and shame that prevents people from reporting these problems.

  - Night eating syndrome: Getting up in the middle of the night to eat.

- Eating problems in people with diabetes are associated with

  - Poor control of diabetes

    - However, a normal A1c does not rule out an eating disorder because A1C is just an average

- It can obscure fluctuations.
- It might also be achieved by unhealthy restrictions.

- Overweight and obesity

- Malnutrition/weight loss

- Impaired psychological well-being

- Repeated hospitalization (Ketoacidosis in Type 1 Diabetes)

- Significant daily blood sugar fluctuations (Roller coaster pattern: recurrent hypoglycemia and high blood sugar levels), which reflects binge eating followed by a severely restricted diet)

The Responsibility of the Doctor

- Weigh these persons less frequently so they don't become distressed by the number, which may trigger the disordered eating behavior.

- Be aware not to push for a low A1C when eating problems are present.

- Seek help from a qualified professional (Psychiatrist/ Psychotherapist)

Referral to a Mental Health Professional (Psychotherapist/ Psychiatrist)

It has been observed that people with diabetes prefer their diabetes health professionals to support them with the emotional aspects of diabetes. However, if the person is experiencing a mental health problem (e.g., eating disorder, major depression, or excessive anxiety), referral to a mental health professional will be necessary. Recent research indicates that a combination of educational, behavioral, and psychological interventional approaches is needed to address stress and control diabetes.

A few commonly used modalities are:

- Supportive psychotherapy
- Motivational interviewing
- Cognitive behavioral therapy includes education, relaxation, coping skills training etc..
- Mindfulness-based therapy
- Family-based behavioral interventions
- Explain the person with diabetes about the reasons for the referral and seek their reactions and thoughts on this step.
- Reassure them that you are interested in their care by continuing to see the person with diabetes after the referral to the mental health professional.
- Check their progress and revise the action plan if you feel it is necessary.
- Maintain communication with the mental health professional to whom the person has been referred and to ensure coordination amongst the entire team.

Conclusion

Emotional health is an important part of the management of diabetes. Stress is a contributing factor to the onset of diabetes as well as a result of having diabetes and managing it. There should be an integration of clinical and emotional care in diabetes.

People with diabetes often struggle to manage the emotions resulting from diabetes management, the fluctuations of blood glucose, the financial cost etc. The day-to-day stress of management affects not just the person with diabetes but the family as well. Stress and emotional factors, if not addressed, result in poor glucose control, more complications and a decreased quality of life.

Reduction of stress and improvement in emotional health improves glucose control, prevents complications and results in an overall better quality of life. This is most effectively achieved by empathic listening by the healthcare provider, educating the person about diabetes, stress and the connection between them, agreement on the goals of treatment, the tasks to be completed to achieve these goals and developing a relationship of trust.

Modalities such as psychotherapy, yoga, meditation and relaxation techniques help individuals prevent or cope with stress and have an important positive effect on the quality of life and glucose control. Certain people may require consultation with a psychiatrist.

There is a great need for understanding the effects of stress, as well as a serious acceptance of the need for psychological support for people with diabetes and in stress. We must realize that people with stress and diabetes are not failing, they are suffering, and they are at great risk. It may be our medical care that is failing to help, recognize, and effectively address their issues, despite strong evidence that the interventions mentioned above help.

A holistic approach that includes the emotional health of people with diabetes is required. Further research should focus on the causes of stress, effects of stress, interventions to reduce stress, as well as benefits of reduction of stress in people with diabetes.

Bibliography

1. Psychosocial Care for People With Diabetes: A Position Statement of the American Diabetes Association Diabetes Care 2016;39:2126–2140

2. Facilitating Positive Health Behaviors and Well-being to Improve Health Outcomes: Standards of Care in Diabetes—2023 Diabetes Care 2023;46 (Suppl. 1):S68–S96

3. Diabetes Self-management Education and Support in Adults With Type 2 Diabetes: A Consensus Report of the American Diabetes Association, the Association of Diabetes Care & Education Specialists, the Academy of Nutrition and Dietetics, the American Academy of Family Physicians, the American Academy of PAs, the American Association of Nurse Practitioners, and the American Pharmacists Association Diabetes Care 2020; 43:1636–1649

4. European Depression in Diabetes (EDID) Research Consortium Pouwer F, et al. Discov Med. 2010. PMID: 20193636 Review

5. Addressing diabetes distress in clinical care: A practical guide Fisher L, Polonsky WH, et al. Diabetic Medicine. 2019:36 803-812.

6. A new look at brittle diabetes J. Diabetes Complications 2021 Jan; 35(1): 107646. Irl B. Hirsch et al.

7. Polonsky WH. Diabetes burnout: what to do if you can't take it anymore. American Diabetes Association; 1999.

8. Facilitating Self-Care in People With Diabetes Richard R. Rubin Diabetes Spectrum Volume 14, Number 2, 2001

9. Anderbro T, Gonder-Frederick L, et al. Fear of hypoglycemia: relationship to hypoglycemic risk and psychological factors. Acta Diabetologica. 2014;52 (3):581-9.

10. Wild D, von Maltzahn R, et al. A critical review of the literature on fear of hypoglycemia in diabetes: implications for diabetes management and patient education. Patient Education and Counseling. 2007;68(1):10-5

11. Identifying solutions to psychological insulin resistance: An international study Polonsky WH, Fisher L, et al. Clinical Diabetes. 2019:33(4) 307-314.

12. Skinner TC, Joensen L, et al. Twenty-five years of diabetes distress research. Diabetic Medicine. 2020;37(3):393-400. European Depression

13. Nefs G, Hendrieckx C, et al. Comorbid elevated symptoms of anxiety and depression in adults with type 1 or type 2 diabetes: Results from the International Diabetes MILES Study. Journal of Diabetes and Its Complications. 2019;33(8):523-29.

14. The confusing tale of depression and distress in patients with diabetes Fisher L, Gonzalez JS, et al. Diabetic Medicine. 2014;31:764-772.

15. Diabetes and anxiety symptoms: a systematic review and meta-analysis Amiri S, Behnazhad S. The International Journal of Psychiatry in Medicine. 2019.

www.ingramcontent.com/pod-product-compliance
Lightning Source LLC
LaVergne TN
LVHW010702200726
843507LV00011B/1968